"Check, Please!"

Designed and written by:

Andrew Bayroff

Designed and written by: Andrew Bayroff
Illustrated by: Sten Ulfsson
Edited by: Carianne Wrona, Michelle McGill

ISBN - 978-0692215814
0692215816

Bragg Street Press

www.CheckPleaseBook.com

Acknowledgments

There are two people I'd like to thank for helping me get this book off the ground; trust me, you'll be thanking them too. First is Sten Ulfsson. He's a talented artist and stand up comedian, and his brilliant illustrations helped bring this book to life. Believe me, his illustrations are far better than my finger paintings. Second, is Carianne Wrona; without her editing and wordsmithing, this book would be a jumble of misspelling and punctuation errors, and honestly, some words I simply made up. So thank you Sten and Carianne!

I'd also like to thank all of the friends and comics who added their own quotes throughout the book: Tory Alan, Sally Dankus, Brian Grossi, Kimberly Manfre, Meredith, Joseph Conklin, Stephen Johnson, Randi, Chris Brooks, Leanne Linsky, Ruthie Kalai, Andrew Lee, Mick Diflo, Charles McBee, Johnny Zito, Christopher Hamilton, Julie Kottakis, and Michelle McGill.

And last, my thanks to all of the women who were the catalyst behind these stories. No names have been mentioned, no personal information has been divulged, so, relax. However, you know who you are ;)

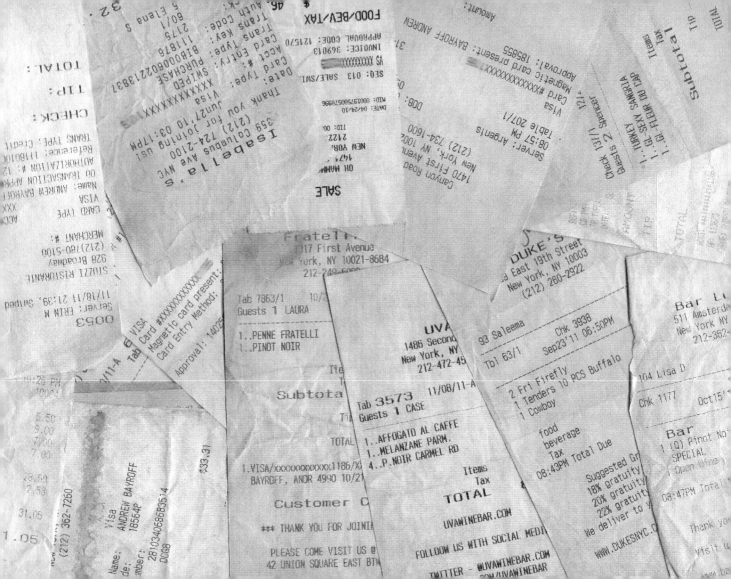

Thanks for buying my book! Or at least picking it up. Maybe you're still thinking you should buy the new Star Wars parody book instead. Or perhaps just save the cash altogether because, who really needs another bathroom book? I hope you make the right decision (to buy this book.) And, come on man, a bathroom book? That hurts.

Check, Please! is filled with my personal dating stories, along with statistics and facts, as well as dating quotes from friends and fellow comics. Each of my dating stories has the inevitable "Needle off the record" moment: that horrid screeching no one can dismiss, when you know full well the date is over and done. You'll know it when you read it.

Over 130 dates

That was my magic number from 2010 to 2013. On average, I spent $40-$50 on a first date. I'm sure some of you are thinking: "$40? You cheap bastard." Easy now, there's a very good explanation for this: I am, in fact, a cheap bastard. Seriously, how is $40 cheap? That's two decent glasses of wine and tip. Who looks good by this math? This guy.

Now, how do I know exactly how many dates I've been on and how much I spent? Simple. I kept the receipts from each date. Why, you ask yourself? Not quite sure myself. I didn't do this as some narcissistic endeavor to prove how good I am or how decent a bloke I've become. As a writer, I figured I'd use the information sooner or later. You can see the receipts in the background throughout the book. And, for those of you who are curious, and would rather not do the math yourself, that's over $6,000 in three years. Seriously? There's a calculator on your phone.

I've been on dates with blonds, brunettes, and redheads. White, Indian, Latin, and other beautiful women. Jews, Catholics, Christians, Atheists, Agnostics. Yoga instructors, educators, lawyers, therapists, business owners, doctors, and artists. Materialistic women, girly-girls, "Mommy & Daddy" types, Alpha Females, snobs, non-TV owners, travelers, and foodies. Marathoners, spontaneous types, planners, do-nothingers, drinkers, pot smokers, museum goers, and hikers. Other than cigarette smokers, I have only two types of women with whom I refuse to go on another date: therapists and lawyers. Look for those chapters later in the book, you'll laugh, you'll cry, you'll plotz.

These pages certainly do not paint a picture of each and every date I have been on. If they did, this book would be the best sleep aid known to man kind. I am only trying to share the stories that stand out in my memory as funny, noteworthy, or just painful. A good many of my dates ended quite harmoniously, no grief, no bad feelings. Sometimes it's simply a nudge nudge, wink wink that silently passes between two people. Saying that it's indeed not a love connection, simply two glasses of wine. However, if all of that energy summons up even the slightest spark, each walks away knowing that there is indeed one more person roaming the streets who also believes that, although Tom Selleck would have made a good Indiana Jones, he was better off as Magnum PI. True story, look it up.

Speaking of wine, I patronized over 130 bars, wine bars, restaurants, bistros and pubs in Manhattan, Queens, and Brooklyn. Have MetroCard, will travel. On page 54, I've listed all, or at least most, of the places I visited on my dates.

Before I leave you, I must talk about The Prep. Most women put a lot of effort into preparing for the date. You know this, and I know this. As any guy might, I appreciate a sweet-smelling, good-looking, well-put-together female. One who obviously put some time, effort, and thought into our first, third, or tenth date. Shower after work, before the date. Clean hair with botanical oils and vitamin extracts, exfoliating body scrub, vanilla body lotion, eyebrows waxed or plucked or threaded, and mani/pedi. That cute little dress you bought at Bloomingdales for a steal, the Jimmy Choo shoes you obtained by threatening the children of women you stole them away from at the latest sale, and lastly, a dash of Coco Mademoiselle that you know will make him weak in the knees.

Sadly, some men are oblivious. After all the showering, primping, spritzing, and pampering you women do for us, and yourselves, we usually look past all of that and simply focus on the ass and boobs. As men, we cannot help it. It's an instinctive, natural reaction. Let me apologize for this.

The closing part

In all honesty, I do hope you enjoy the book and that it finds a comfortable place on your shelf, or coffee table. Let's face it, this is going in your bathroom. Hopefully all of you can see the comedy in these stories as I do, and learn from them. Or at least write a book that your mother will purchase.

Contents

Waiter. Check, Please!

"Do you need a TOWEL, or perhaps a shower?"

"Oh Andrew. Your shirt feels so dry and absorbent."

his query ran through my head as soon as we sat down for our first date coffee.

She was attractive, beautiful smile, long brunette hair...and sweating. Profusely. I knew she would be meeting me after her yoga class, but, silly me, I figured she'd clean up a bit, change her clothing, or at least change her shirt.

She made light of the fact that she "just came from yoga", as she smiled at me. Really, you just came from working out? Not sure what gave it away. Perhaps the yoga mat under your arm, or maybe the fresh the "glow" of sweat across your entire body.

Listen, I'm a yoga fan, Vinyasa for 2+ years, and I love what it has done for my body and mind. If it was indeed a Bikram (hot yoga) class, I'm sure she got a great workout; however, I've never arrived minutes from class to a first date, with a cupful of sweat sheening my body, depleted water bottle, and toting what can only be an equally drenched yoga mat that smelled like a circus bathroom.

The coffee was delicious, the pastry tasty, and she just wouldn't stop talking about how amazing her yoga class was and that she "really worked up a sweat."

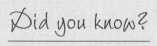

Offhandedly, I mentioned, "My club offers towels before each class." She kept sipping her coffee and smiling. I attempted to steer the conversation away from yoga, however. No matter how hard I tried, she pulled a U-turn and came right back to her favorite position. Happy Baby in case you were wondering.

She was sweet, but if this is even a small looking-glass into a potential future, I say good Downward Dog to you, m'lady. She gave me a sweaty hug good bye, and in doing so, I was exposed to the full aroma of an hour-long yoga class. It was not pleasant, and I'd rather stop talking about it.

Namaste, *Check Please!*

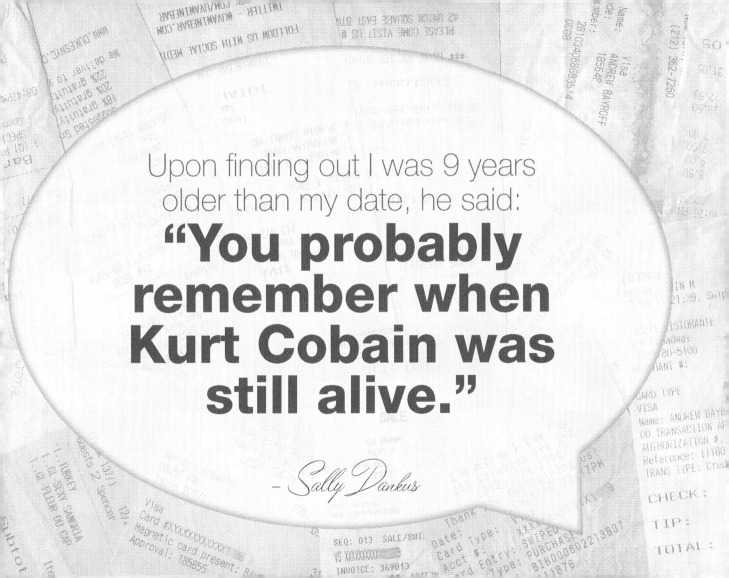

Upon finding out I was 9 years older than my date, he said:

"You probably remember when Kurt Cobain was still alive."

— Sally Dankus

"I'm currently smoking my fourth husband in this one."

**I** have cats. There, I said it. Dates have told me they are allergic to cats, dislike cats, and some have gone so far as to tell me they hate cats. Hate, because they saw a cat hiss in a Stephen King movie once. Some even ask me, "Why, don't you like dogs?" No, I hate dogs. In fact, since I have cats, I hate all other living creatures. Including those cute pandas we watch having sex at the zoo.

The very worst comment I received was at the end of a date that tragically ended 30 minutes after it started. I turned to the woman and asked: "What do you think about pets?" Notice, no mention of cats. Her response: "I fucking hate cats. I think they are disgusting."

Me-yow!

She saw by the look on my face that in fact I did own cats, to which her response was: "Oh God, you own cats? Why? They are so fucking filthy."

Back off guys, she's all mine.

This came from a girl who not only wore a low neckline leopard-print top, but enough perfume to choke (and then decompose) a horse. She also told me numerous times that she was a heavy pot smoker, and explained that she broke off an engagement 'cause, "He didn't understand that I like smoking pot and that I would be doing so well into my 60's." On the outside I was expressionless, nodding and trying to see her point of view. However, on the inside, I was already home watching reruns of the West Wing. (People tell me I remind them of the Will Bailey character.)

I have nothing against pot or pot smokers, however. Basing your reason for breaking off an engagement because of your pot intake is the same as hating cats because one looked at you wrong when you were 5-years old. It makes you look like an idiot.

As the night slowly and painfully progressed, she began to explain each piece of her jewelry, what it meant to her, and who gave it to her: "This was from an ex-boyfriend, my parents, my fiancée, a trip to Italy, and my parents."

Obviously her not enjoying the company of a cat was just one reason I never asked her out again. Whoever does marry her, and her collection of bongs given to her by various men, you have my deepest sympathies. And if you have glaucoma, all the best.

Here kitty kitty, *Check Please!*

"I see the bill, but I'm not sure how I *feel* about it."

 **W**ords that five minutes before had a completely different meaning.

See, my date was a therapist, as were her father, mother, brother, uncle, aunt, and next door neighbor's dog walker on her mother's side.

"So You Say," turned out to be her personal mantra in life. Someone would tell her it would be impossible to get the job she just interviewed for, she would promptly, and a bit too smugly, respond, "So you say." Meaning, everything is possible, and just because you say it isn't, doesn't make it so. I actually appreciate the sentiment.

However, practical application doesn't always work. See, there are times it's not what "I say," it's what others do. For instance, when Mila Kunis' bodyguard tells me I will not be allowed in her dressing room to get a lock of her hair, I leave or risk having a lock of my body removed. Or even if my mind wants to raise money for a worthy charity by walking to the top of the Empire State Building, my body chimes in and offers a succinct: I don't think so, old man.

I tried drumming up casual date conversation, talking about where she grew up, schools she went to and her advanced training. That not only didn't add to the effort, but detracted. Sometimes topics

Did you know?

Thirty-three percent of online daters form a relationship, 33% do not, and 33% give up.

Four out of ten workplace dating relationships result in marriage.

It only takes seconds to decide another person's attractiveness.

9%
Women who find relationships at a bar

are best left untouched, and allowed to slumber in the corner of the bar. I have yet to learn this skill. Sad for me, fun for you!

She told me she recently took part in what she liked to call a "Leadership Program." Wherein you would not only live with the other "Cadets" in a dorm-style building, but you would be on-call, day and night, to carry out specific projects sent down from high atop the "So You Say" food chain. I knew the date was over when she told me participants in the program could likely be in the very bar in which we were sitting. Monitoring. Part of one of their assignments. I started to hear, "We are Borg, resistance is futile," over and over in my head.

The bill came and we both looked at each other. She reminded me that the man usually pays for the first date. With a straight face I looked at her and said, "So you say."

So I say, *Check Please!*

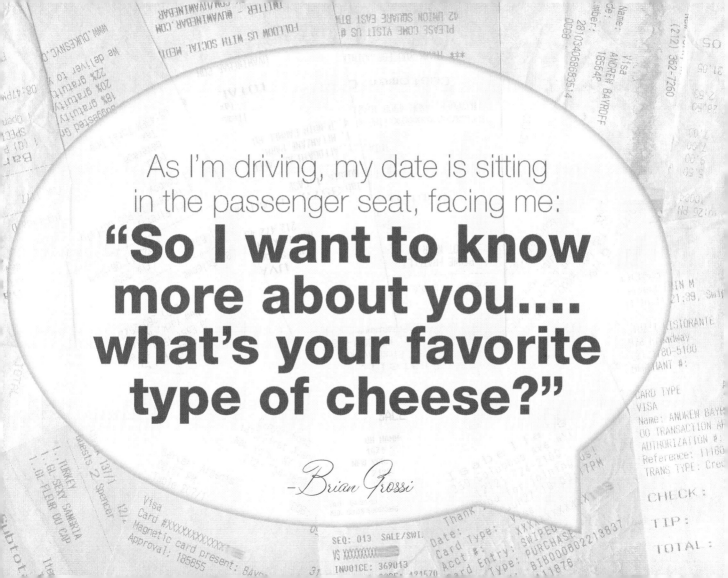

As I'm driving, my date is sitting in the passenger seat, facing me: "So I want to know more about you.... what's your favorite type of cheese?"

—Brian Grossi

" Would you
like to be
ALONE
with your phone? **"**

"My friend keeps texting that her date isn't paying attention to her. So rude."

question I should have asked right away. But I let her nervous tic continue. Picking up the phone, looking at the screen, putting it down, repeated over and over again. I figured she was either waiting for a call from the office, or the glow of the screen made her happy.

Things that are considered bad form when on a date:

1. Emailing
2. Texting
3. Talking on the phone
4. Updating your Facebook status
5. Taking selfies with the hunky bartender
6. Removing shoes and socks and rubbing your feet
7. Clipping your finger and/or toenails
8. Ordering top-shelf liquor, tasting it, then telling the bartender you don't like how it tickles your nose

After about the 5th or 6th time she checked her phone, I asked her if everything was okay. When pressed for an answer, this flower of a date informs me: "I'm sorry. I'm waiting to hear from the guy I buy my pot from. He's going to tell me where to meet him." She smiled, and returned her attention to the glow of her smart phone.

Did you know?

Typically, dating specialists suggest waiting until the third date to cook someone dinner at home.

Studies show that happiness is contagious and that potential dates find it hard to walk away from happy people.

To create an instant link with a date, say his or her name at least twice in the conversation. This shows attentiveness and connectiveness.

2%
Men who find relationships at a bar

I'm a grown man, ladies and gentlemen. I've lived in many cities, partied with some cool people. Hell, I've even been heckled on stage, but never have I had a date interrupted because of weed delivery. Because I've said something inappropriate, sure. But never for drug delivery.

Alas, a long-term relationship was thwarted before it had time to sprout wings, grow feathers, and whisk us both to the far-off land called Love. Turns out she was a heavy drinker and even heavier cigarette smoker. And as I've already stated, I don't do well with smokers. I had no issue with the pot, it was her neurotic, nay, obsessive-compulsive hand-twitching in checking her phone lest she missed the all-important call.

We walked to Union Square from the bar; it was snowing. After I gave her what I like to call "the non-hug" she blurts out: "This was fun, we should do it again." I laughed and walked down the subway stairs.

Toke 'em if you got 'em, *Check Please!*

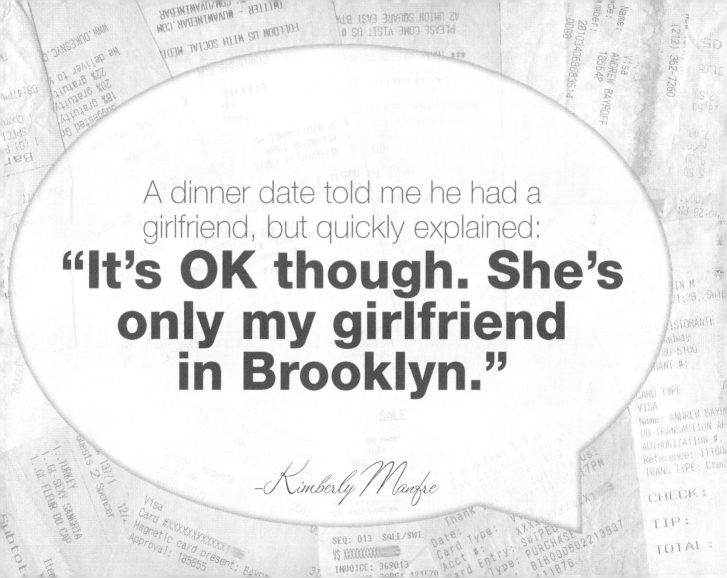

A dinner date told me he had a girlfriend, but quickly explained:

"It's OK though. She's only my girlfriend in Brooklyn."

—Kimberly Manfre

"I decided to go to my family's BEACH HOUSE instead"

"Hey, it's Andrew. I've got a great seat at brunch. You almost here?"

**N**ot the most common reason a woman would cancel the date, I guess I'm one of the lucky ones.

I met this beautiful girl online, Match I believe. She actually reached out to me first, saying she enjoyed my profile and asking me, "wanna chat?" A small handful of emails later we were talking on the phone. Conversation went very well, had a lot in common, blah blah blah.

We hit it off as much as you can in an hour's conversation. Not sure what it was about her though, but I was intrigued by this woman. Good sense of humor, professional, with the right amount of sarcasm. She would see me in a newly pressed shirt, one with the dry cleaning tag removed right before the date. Yeah, she was dry cleaner tag good.

After commenting that I was free on Saturday, she said, "sounds good," and to contact her Saturday morning to make plans. I did just that and texted her around 10 A.M.: *"Hey there, morning. How about we grab some brunch in SoHo, Upper West Side? Talk soon."*

About twenty minutes later I received this text: "Hi Andrew. I actually decided to go to my family's beach house instead. How about we pick some other day?" On the advice from a cousin of mine (she's a clinical psychologist) I texted Ms. Beach House in return: "OK, sounds good. Hope I get to see you before your tan wears off ;)"

Something about sending that second text did not sit right with me. When my cousin texted me again, recanting her previous message, I knew my Spidey Sense didn't fail me. She said that it was indeed rude, and not to text the would-be date back. After explaining to my dear cousin that I in fact had already texted the woman, plus, used her cute suggestion, she told me: "Well, look at it this way, you come out of this looking like the adult."

Now, I've looked like an ass, the "good guy," I've even looked confused. However, if there's one thing I was hoping from meeting this woman, it was not the hope to come out looking like the adult.

Oh Cabana Boy, *Check Please!*

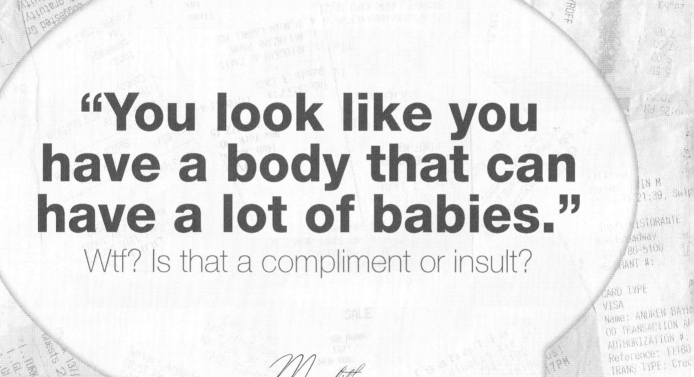

"You look like you have a body that can have a lot of babies."

Wtf? Is that a compliment or insult?

—Meredith

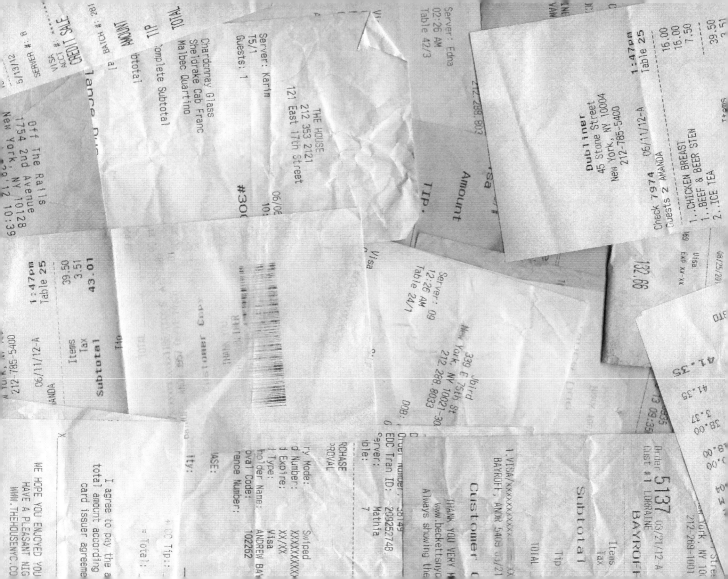

**"He had a
GIRLFRIEND,
but I didn't care"**

"You're already dating someone, great! What's your position on STDs?"

This gem was uttered in the middle of what I can at best describe as a sort-of-date: We sort of knew each other. I sort of was enjoying myself. She sort of showed signs of being a human being.

We sat in the back room of a lounge, not too crowded, decent music. I ordered the chicken strips, she, a bowl of edamame. As we talked, she meticulously picked each bean from the bowl, and gently placed it in her mouth.

As she talked in semi-coherent sentences, I gathered a few spits and spats of clues about what she did and where she's traveled. We started discussing online dating in NYC.

As we dipped deeper into the conversation, and my chicken into the BBQ sauce, I quickly realized she may not be The One for me. Seems a guy having a girlfriend didn't really bother her, since she "wasn't looking for anything long-term." She divulged she recently fooled around with a guy who was already in a committed relationship, and the girlfriend had no idea. At this point in my head I was thinking the couple needed to revisit the true definition of "committed relationship." She also added, listen up everyone, she may "need to get tested."

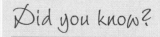

Did you know?

An average couple will kiss on the second date

Twenty-nine percent of Americans have had sex on the first date.

A woman can increase the likelihood of a man approaching her if she uncrosses her arms, makes subtle eye contact, and smiles.

80%
Men that date women that are at least 5 years younger than them

And another edamame is dead.

When the check was placed dead center on the table — I was not planning on asking her for cash, mind you — she looked at me and said: "I never really offer to pay, sorry." With a shrug of her shoulder, she popped another bean in her mouth and sat listening to the music.

And quicker than Clark Kent changing in a bathroom stall at Grand Central, we were street bound. A quick hug and I descended into the NYC subway system. The girl? Hopefully off to an urgent care for a blood test.

Excuse me, doctor, *Check Please!*

A collage of overlapping, crumpled restaurant receipts at various orientations.

MARUZZELLA (upside down, upper left)
- SALAD
- SALAD
- Taxable:
- 17.00
- 16.50
- 2 SLASS HAMBURGER GUESTS 2
- 35.25
- 9.50
- 3.97
- 17.75
- 17.50
- MANAGER MONTER
- FOOD
- BeveragesTAX
- 1 PENNE VODKA
- 1 GLASS MONTEP
- TABLE 14
- 16:12 D 08/10/12
- Total
- SubTotal

Felice Wine Bar (center)
- 1166 First Avenue
- New York, NY 10065
- (212) 593-2223
- SALE
- BAR #1
- XXXXXXXXX
- card prese

Bocca E (left center)
- 1496 2nd
- New York, NY
- Aug19,1
- Date:
- Card Type: Visa
- Card #: XXX
- Acct #: SMI
- Card Entry: PUR
- Trans Type: 165
- th Code:
- eck: 189
- Check ID: B1
- Server: 403

Eataly (right center)
- 200 Fifth Avenue
- New York, NY 10010
- Dolcetto
- Rose
- glass
- 1 Margarita Glass-
- rock
- 1 Braised sh rib---
- charedtomato
- SUB TOTAL:
- Tax 1:
- AMOUNT DUE:
- 6/27/20

Café - 7 DAYS (top right)
- Cust. 2 Server 24 All H
- :34 PM Check 266210
- Sub-total:
- Tax:
- Due: 36.50
- Taxable: 33.50
- Tax: 3.00
- 33.50
- 31.00
- 7.00
- 11.00
- 6.00
- 1.08
- 1.43
- eck 154378
- ber 10 Olivia
- 7/28/201
- 07/06

#41

V BAR ST MARKS (bottom left)
- 31 Second Avenue
- New York, NY 10003
- Tel. 212.473.7200
- V Bar
- V Bar
- 11/21/12
- XXXXXX / ANDRE

Gravy NY (bottom center)
- 32 East 21st St
- New York, NY
- 212-600-2105
- Table #107
- 19244
- 9/25/2012 11:38 PM
- Serv: Gaelan # Cust
- Duan Descript
- Patron Cafe XO
- -10
- Net

(bottom right)
- 928 Broadway
- New York, NY 10010
- (212) 780-5100
- Thank you for dining with us!
- Tax:
- 33.

" I'm looking for someone to TAKE CARE of me "

"This one looks good I guess. Let's see the front."

**S**tart your engines ladies and gentlemen, this is going to be a fun ride!

This "relationship" spanned nearly a year. This was one of those 2-months-on, 4-months-off, 3-months-on, type of exchanges.

We originally found each other online (it's a running theme) and hit it off right away. Thing is, even though our time together was pleasant, and we were definitely attracted to each other, everything seemed to be one-sided from the start. She always waited for me to ask her out each time, even once we passed the "courting" stage. She never contacted me to make plans, ever. I'm all for the guy lighting the fuse, letting the gal know he's interested, but somewhere along the line ladies, you own a phone and email address, clickity-click.

On our third attempt at a relationship, she texted me 20 minutes before I was set to leave to meet her. She had a family emergency and was sorry, but she had to cancel. I immediately texted back not to worry, it's your family, go do what you need to. She then promptly replied, "thank you." That was the last I heard from her until maybe four months later when we "found" each other, again, and began what would be our last attempt.

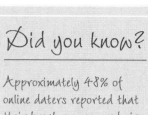

Did you know?

Approximately 48% of online daters reported that their breakups occurred via email.

eHarmony.com boasts that 236 of its members marry each day, accounting for 2% of U.S. marriages.

Over half of all singles in America have not had a date in over two years.

12%
Chance after a first date a guy will call if he hasn't called within 24 hours

Let me pause here for a second and revisit what I mentioned earlier in the book: paying for the date. In what I can only imagine was a solid 15 dates, including everything from wine and dinner to dessert, Broadway show and taxis; she paid for one bottle of beer. Never offered, flinched, nudged, or even flickered to offer to add in for the bill.

It was on what would be our last date when I became very curious. I simply asked her, "Well, tell me, what is it that you are looking for?" With no sense of shyness, she responded, "I am looking for someone to take care of me." In no uncertain terms, she was talking financially.

In the end she was looking for a sugar daddy. I'm a comic, I'm barely Sweet and Low. I could have easily shown her my bank account balance and immediately dispense with the idea of her quitting her day job and hiring three nannies for the impending children. Then again, pain fuels comedy. I probably would have smashed my foot with a hammer for inspiration.

When the bill came and one of my credit cards was declined (I forgot to activate it) she simply sat there, checking her email. I gave the young waiter a different card and we left.

Excuse me, Visa, *Check Please!*

My date pointed to his phone and says:

"I have wanted to hook up with this guy for a while, he just messaged me. Can we take a rain check?"

—Stephen Johnson

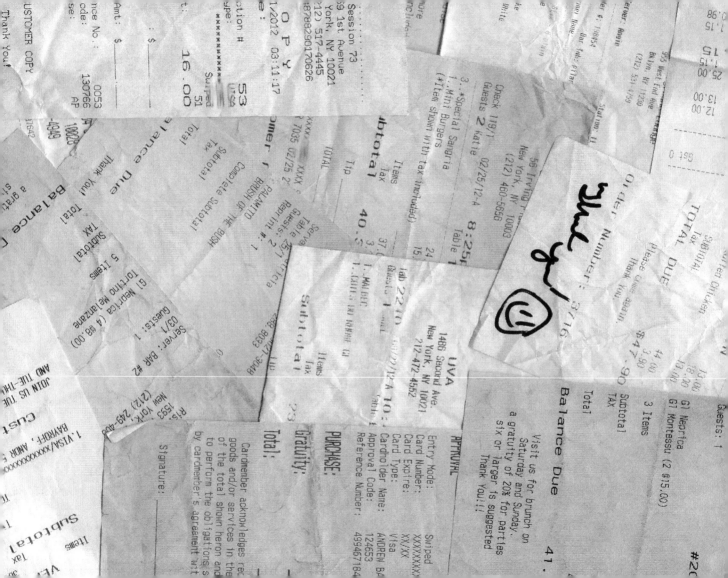

" My
BOYFRIEND
loved that movie **"**

"It's OK. My boyfriend loves when I touch random guys. He's actually watching us right now."

o be fair, this was not a date. I stopped in at a local bar to have a drink and some food, and started chatting to the woman to my left. Casual conversation, commenting on whatever was on the TV, the usual chatter. Then, harmless light touches on my arm.

As we drank our beer and ate our food, the conversation become a bit more personal, where are you from, siblings, kids, all the type of information that gives guys that tingly feeling in the pit of their stomach that says, "I'm gonna get some!"

I'm thinking, if I ask her out she'll most likely say yes. So, I tried to choose wisely, like Indiana Jones, and wait for a lull in the conversation. However, when a commercial for a Sci-Fi movie came on she blurted out: "Oh man. My boyfriend loved that movie." It may have been for the re-re-release of the Star Wars Trilogy.

I sorta...just...sat there. I smiled, as not to bring the conversation to a screeching halt. "Oh, boyfriend a big Sci-Fi fan?" Not sure why I asked; from her bellowing tone, he obviously was, indeed, a fan of the Science Fiction. We sat there, watching the commercial together, as I wondered, what in the hell just happened? Was this Candid Camera? Am I, Andrew Bayroff, being Punk'd?

Did you know?

A man's top dating fears include that a woman will come between him and his friends, won't allow him free time, will turn out to be a stalker, won't respect him, or will be too high maintenance.

If a group of women are standing together but their eyes are wandering, they are likely to be looking for guys.

25%

Percent of single people that say touching as a way to flirt and is very effective

We chatted for a bit more, but I kept it a very surface conversation, work, vacations, flirting with seemingly single women at bars. The normal list. She continued to be as flirty as before, I allowed it to happen. Let's face it, I'm a man. We really don't care either way.

She gave me a hug goodbye before she left, which left me more confused. I had to conclude: 1. I was indeed part of some Web "Candid Camera" episode, 2. She does this for shits and giggles, or 3. Eh, who the hell cares. I got a hug :)

The Chalmun Cantina is now closed, *Check Please!*

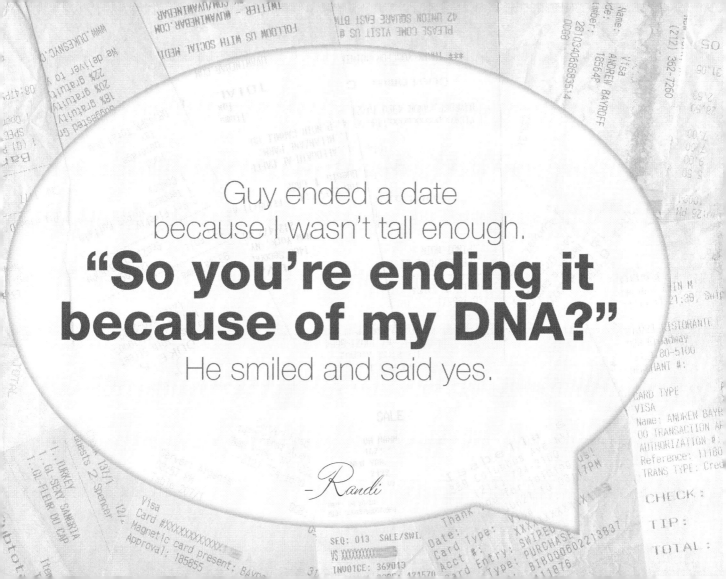

AUGUST RESTAURANT
359 BLEECKER ST
359 Bleecker St.
212-929-4774

Server: Susanna
Cashier: Amanda
Table 64/1
Guests: 2

Mimosa   6.0
Coffee   7.5
Eggs Coccotte

Items   39.1
Tax   3.5
TOTAL   43.0

THE HOUSE
212 353 21
121 East 17th

ver: Dru
close/1

Jbird
339 E 75th St
New York, NY 10021-3048
212.288.8033

09/22/20
10-09

BREEZE FIZZ

3, Gimal 20 FL, padwS 'Ot'00

Balance Due

Thank You!

New York, NY
212.288.8033

Server: BARTENDER
50/1   09.59 PM

Visa
Card #XXXXXXXXXX
Magnetic Card Method
Card Entry Method

Approval: 1357   SALE

---

1. TURKEY
2. GL - MALBEC
2. GL RIESLING

1040   [BT1] Dine
Aileen

AmBer
1466 third ave
New York, NY 10022
Tel 212.249.5020

AMBER AVE
3RD   NY 10075

---

1. VISA/xxxxxxxxxxxx
2. xxxx S A:10515
ANDREW BAYRUF 2032 04/25 21:59   60.9

Customer Copy

JOIN US FOR FREE PANINI MONDAYS AND OUR
NEW $5 SANGRIA HAPPY HOUR, TUES-FRI FROM
4PM-7PM, AND ALL DAY SUNDAY!!!

Subtotal   60.9
Tax
Items
Tip
TOTAL

Trailer Park Lounge
271 West 23rd. Street
10011 New York
Phone 212-463-8000

0111 - 35792

Grilled Chicken Sandwich   10.95
Grilled Cheese Sandwich   10.70
                             4.50

                            26.15
                           $ 2.32
                           28.47

Balance Due

Thank you
Please Join us ag
Please inquire
Catering Avai

Ot Txonin Etxanitz
Croquette/Chips
Mushrooms

Complete Subtotal
Subtotal
Tax
Total

"I ordered food while you were in the BATHROOM"

*"Wait a second. They don't even **serve** lobster here!"*

My female friends love this first date story, and so will you. Unless you're the first date, and if so, thank you, thank you, thank you.

We met for our first date at a, you guessed it, wine bar. Hug, cheek kiss, and we took our seat at the bar. As we talked, she asked me, "Are you hungry?" I told her to take a look at the menu and we'll see what's good. I excused myself and went to the bathroom, an exercise that took a total of 63 seconds; I actually washed my hands.

This is when things took a downturn for the date, but an upturn for this book. Upon my return she asked me, "Do you like veal?" I said not at all. "What about pork?" Nope, not so much. Turns out she's an aspiring chef, a self-proclaimed "foodie" she repeated multiple times. And if you're like me, the sheer mention of that word makes you uncomfortable. Like a single guy at a pre-teen fashion show.

I soon realized why the query about my taste buds. Soon after my return, a plate of veal meatballs and a pulled pork plate were set in front of us; which she slowly slid to her side of the bar. Turns out, during my extended excursion, she took it upon herself to order food while I was in the bathroom. She ordered food while I was in the bathroom! That's the equivalent of me putting a condom on before the date starts. Since I was away from the table for more than 30 seconds, I can completely understand her lack of patience to wait for me. After the tense five seconds of shock were over, she proceeded to eat all the food and drink three glasses of wine.

I was torn, pulled rather, like the pork. I liked her, she was attractive, funny and intelligent. However, ordering food while your date is in the bathroom? It's not like she ordered a salad, or chips and a nice dip, but pork and veal? Two meats that, although popular, may not be on the top of the list of dietary choices for a lot of people.

As I watched her drink her glasses of wine and devour her meat, I sat there and thought to myself: She's definitely not showing enough cleavage to get away with this crap.

Her total on the bill: $65, mine, $16.

Bathroom attendant, *Check Please!*

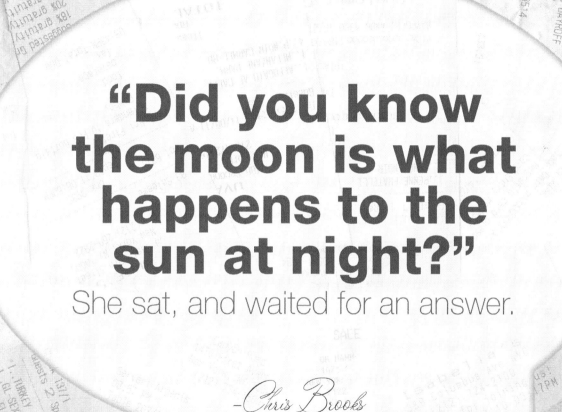

"Did you know the moon is what happens to the sun at night?"

She sat, and waited for an answer.

-Chris Brooks

Semi complete list of dating locations between 2010 and 2013

2010
Dive 75
Arte Cafe
Vino
Haakons Hall
Totonno's
Forum
Amedeo Buenoa Sera Cor
Sur La Table
Bar Luna
Wine and Roses x2
Le Pain Quotidien
Gracie Mews Diner
Boat Basin
Le Colonial x2
Viand
Felice, 116 First Ave x2
Tre
Veselka
Gine La Fornarina
Brother Jimmy's x3
Side Bar x2
Blue Moon

Vero
Bowlmor Lanes
Belmont Lounge
American Trash
El Cantenero
Agata & Valentina
Landmarc

2011
Punch
Wine & Roses
Felice x3
Side Bar
AOC
The Cupping Room
Amsterdam Ale House
Fratelli's
Garcias
Hillstone
Boat Basin
Gottino
Tre
Stuzzi Ristorante'Isabella's

Oh Mamma Mia x2
One and One
Canyon Road
Vero
Bar Luna
Bar Veloce x4
Duke's
Uva
Sanctuary T
Forino Park Slope x2
Lillie's
Salumeria Rosi
Cello Wine Bar
Canyon Road
Nectar
Belmont Lounge x3
Cava Wine Bar
El Paso Tarueria x2
Blackstones
Pier 66 Maritime
Jane
Barcioo Enoteca
Vino

Slice
Monaco
Vero
Motorino
Reservoir Bar
Stir x2
Baraonda
Gravy
Southern Hospitality
Igloo
Bocca di bacco
The Campbell
Garage Restaurant

2012
The House x3
Baraonda
Cafe Wha
Beach cafe
Stuzzi Ristoriante
Pepe Patron
Eataly
Wilfie & Nell
Gravy x2
Maruzzella
V Bar St. Marks

Bocca East
Felice
Bar Veloce East
Vero x3
Epicerie Boulud
Central Bar
JBird x6
Pig 'n' Whistle
Cilantro
August Restaurant
Amber
Trailer Park Lounge
Buceo
The GingerMan
The Underground Lounge
Brandy's Piano Bar
Cibar
Felice 1593 First Ave x2
Session 73
Citrus
Uva x2
Cavatappo Wine Bar
Aza
Dresner's Restaurant
Roman's
Baraonda

Off The Rails
Dubliner
Cava Wine Bar
Beckett's
Dubliner
Vino

2013
Maya
Barcibo Enoteca x2
The House
The Malt House
Dakota Bar
Cilantro
Big Daddy's
Fratelli's x2
Bocca x2
Solo Trattoria
Bar Olivino
Brandys Piano Bar
Boat Basin
Uva
Johnny Foxes
Gravy

And what are you spending on your first date?[3]

You may be reading this book in Houston, perhaps Los Angeles, or maybe you're still in a store in Atlanta but haven't quite decided to buy this book, or the new copy of the TV Guide. Either way, what do you usually spend on a first date? $50, $75, maybe even $100? New York seems to be at the tail end, but it's all uphill from there. Women, I know you offer money, and sometimes even mean it. For now though, we'll concentrate on the guys out there.

This book is not about money, however. Fellow New Yorkers, am I alone in thinking $145 is a bit much for a first date? Not to mention $221! Colorado, we all want to show our ladies a good time, but does it need to cross the $200 mark on the very first date? I break men down into three different categories when it comes to first dates and shelling out some cash:

1. You're pulling in a damn good paycheck, kudos for you
2. You believe in the courting process, because your mama raised you right
3. Your date continues to order food or suggest activities and you can't say no
(4. To get laid)

How does the rest of the readers out there stack up? Let the world know at: www.CheckPleaseBook.com

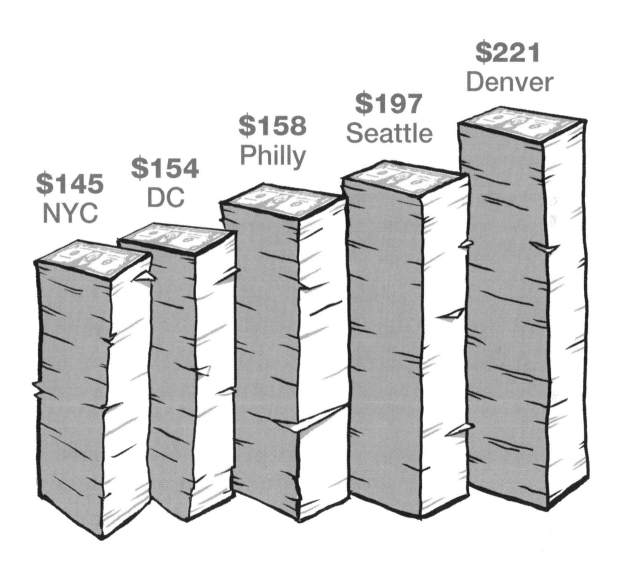

1.. W Vega Sindoa
Vega Sindo GLASS
1.. W Cune Vinas Crnz
Cune Vinas GLASS
1.. D Spring Rolls
1.. D sm Shrmp Risoto

Items
Tax
TOTAL

Join Us at Punch for Ha
everyday from 4-8
&
Happy Hour @ Wine
from 5-8pm

1166 First Avenue
New York, NY 10065
(212) 593-2223

DOB:

SALE

Server: BAR #1
11:05 PM
BB 82/1

VISA
Card #XXXXXXXXXXX
Magnetic card present: BAYROFF
Card Entry Method: S

Approval: 140256

Amount:

+ Tip:

= Total:

I agree to pay the
total amount accordin
card issuer agreer

Felice is open everyday
a gratuity of 20% for
six or larger is s
Thank You!

X

GUESTS COP

Table:
0104 Cabernet Franc   14.0
23 Chix Panini
MESSAGE
no stilton
MESSAGE
Sub Agtz
12 Salad Arugula
MESSAGE
sub rocket panin
MESSAGE
no queso azul
Americano
Cappuccino
43 Cheese Cake

SUBTOTAL
Tax Tax
Incl DUE
TOTAL Thank Y

259 FIFTH AVENUE
BROOKLYN, NY 11215
TEL 1-718-788-1519

able 102
#a guest 2
WAITERS

1 LA MAITRESSE
1 HALF CHICKEN FRITE
1 IRON GRILL

Sub Total
TAX 8 875%

TOTAL

FOOD   6.90
LIQUORS

For your convenience
15% Gratuity = 6.90
18% Gratuity = 8.28
20% Gratuity = 9.20

Visa
Card #XXXXXXXXXX
Magnetic card prese
Approval: 07761A

X

Tha
Side Bar -
Vintage Irvin

>>Custor

10/21/11-A 9:03pm
Table B-03

Items   16.95
              11.00

Total 27.95
Tax   2.34

Total 30.29

Tip

TOTAL

Customer Copy

FOR JOINING US ***

VISIT US @ PIZZA BASH
RE EAST BTWN 16-17 ST

SALE
XX/XXXX S A:142990
990 10/21 21:29 30.29

ACCOUNT
XXXXXXX
BAYROFF
ON APPROVED
N #: 124634
118010XXX053
Credit Card SALE

SPECIAL
VISA

TIP AMOUNT

TOTAL

12-249-6092

erdam Ale House
Amsterdam Avenue
York, NY 10018
(212) 362-7260

er:
281034066635
0CG8

Visa
ANDREW BAYR
18564P

The Cupping Room Cafe
www.cuppingroomcafe.com
359 West Broadway, Soho
New York, NY 10013
1 212-925-2898

Server: 8am
Table 12/1
Guests: 2
Reprint #: 1

12/31
5:20
30C8

Iced Tea
Diet Coke
Tuna Melt Sandwich
Eggs
Sausage
Cafe Latte
Strawberry Cheese Cake

Sub Total
Tax

cknow
serv*
sho*

Sub Total

"It makes me feel more LIKE A WOMAN"

"I'd rather **you** lay down in the puddle instead."

This line of crap came on the third date after a night of food, drinks, and live comedy. We stopped at a bar before calling it a night, a glass of wine each and some good chatter.

Before I left the bar to go to the bathroom, she said "Ok, I'll get the check." I'm thinking great, she'll pay so we can leave as soon as I come back. Silly me, upon my return, I realized she didn't pay the bill, she simply asked for the bill.

As I started to put my jacket on, she announces, "Sweetie, do you think you paid, cause you didn't yet," and proceeded to slide the bill in my direction. I swear I wish I was making this up. Let me say that up until and including the third date, I had planned and paid for everything. Not bragging, just stating a fact.

On the taxi ride uptown (God forbid she agreed to take the subway) she asked me if something was wrong. I said, "You couldn't have put down a twenty at the bar?" And here's her response: "I was thinking about paying, but I guess I'm just Old-fashioned. When a man pays for me it makes me feel like a woman."

That void you're feeling right now? That lack of response or retort, is exactly how I felt as soon as the words came out of her mouth, and rattled around in my brain. I wouldn't be surprised if at some point she'd demand I lay my coat down for her in the rain. I actually never understood how stepping on someone's coat was chivalrous. It's raining, what is my knock-off 1985 Member's Only jacket going to protect you from?

However, looking at her was akin to staring at a beautiful piece of artwork. You get so lost in the beauty that you simply forget what the hell you were thinking just moments ago. The hair. The skin. The Old-fashioned farm jokes that were now bouncing around in my head. Part of me waited for her to say "Just kidding!", but alas, my hope for a comical interlude was thwarted by a smirk and a small hug.

The term Old-fashioned used to mean something. Opening the door for her, pulling the chair out for her, asking her father's permission for marriage. If she were so "Old-fashioned," maybe I simply should have brought her father a chicken and a couple of cows and called it a day.

Moo, *Check Please!*

"It's just a ring my ex-wife gave me. It just makes sense to wear it on the ring finger."

On first, and last, date with a guy.

-Leanne Linksy

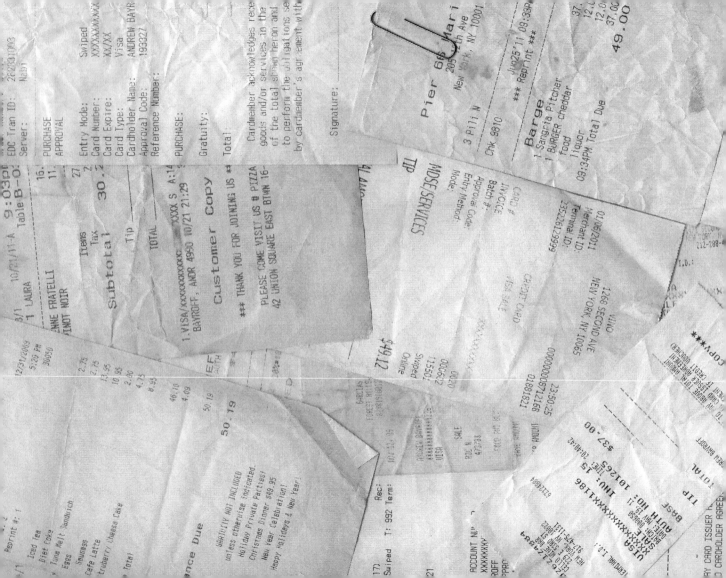

EDC Tran ID: 26283003
Server: Nabi

PURCHASE
APPROVAL

Entry Mode: Swiped
Card Number: XXXXXXXXX
Card Expire: XX/XX
Card Type: Visa
Cardholder Name: ANDREW BAYR
Approval Code: 193327
Reference Number:

PURCHASE:

Gratuity:

Total:

Cardmember acknowledges rece
goods and/or services in the
of the total shown heron and
to perform the obligations se
by cardmember's agreement with

Signature:

Pier 66 Mari
205 12th Ave
New York, NY 10001

*** Jue25'11 09:33P
*** Reprint ***

3 Pili N

Chk 9810
09:34PM

Barge
1 Sangria Pitcher
1 BURGER cheddar
food
liquor
09:34PM Total Due

37.
12.0
12.0
37.00

49.6

9:03P
Table B-0

8/1   10/21/11-A

ANNE FRATELLI
1 PINOT NOIR   16.
11.

Items   27
Tax   2
Subtotal   30.2

Tip _____

TOTAL _____

1 VISA/xxxxxxxxxxxx XXXX S A:14
BAYROFF, ANDR 4990 10/21 21:29

Customer Copy

*** THANK YOU FOR JOINING US **
PLEASE COME VISIT US @ PIZZA
42 UNION SQUARE EAST BTWN 16-

MDSE/SERVICES

TIP

CARD #
INVOICE
Batch #
Approval Code
Entry Method
Mode:

Terminal ID: 735524
Merchant ID: 6666781873

01/06/201

1266 SECOND AVE
NEW YORK, NY 10065

CREDIT CARD
VISA SALE

XXXXXXXXX

212-788-

1.0.

Online
Swiped   1150
0060   0000
0200

23:50:25   23318810

$21.4

Reprint #: 1

12/31/2009
5:26 PM
30050

Iced Tea   2.75
Diet Coke   2.75
Tuna Melt Sandwich   11.95
Eggs   10.95
Sausage   2.90
Cafe Latte   4.75
Strawberry Cheese Cake   8.99

Total   46.10
4.09

50.19

50.19

Balance Due

GRATUITY NOT INCLUDED
Unless otherwise indicated.
Holiday Private Parties!
Christmas Dinner $89.95
New Year Celebration!
Happy Holidays & New Year!

Rec:

T: 992 Term:

Swiped

GARCIA,
TOMAS MELIS

XXXXXXXXXX
SALE
VISA
REC #: 473/33

*** Vv****
COPY
REQUIRED

ACCOUNT N
XXXXXXXX
ROFF
PPRT

VISA XXXXXXXXX1186
XXXXX SALE
ROFF
1.0.

NEW YORK NY
917-473-1181

TECHNICAL 1.0.

TOTAL
TIP
BASE $37.00

INV: 15   TIME: 20:40:42
AUTH NO: 10126S
DATE: MAY 19 11
SALE

$37.00

RY CARD ISSUER H
D CARDHOLDER AGREE

DREW BAYROFF

"I **NEVER** take the subway"

"Don't worry, the trains are clean. The rats are pretty friendly, too."

S omeone who meant well thought her friend and I would be a great match. She, a luxury goods executive, and me, a guy who embraces everything about mass transit.

As we talked on the phone, she asked where I worked. At the time, my office was near Wall St. "I take the subway to lower Manhattan, not a bad ride." Which is when she released, "Oh, I never take the subway, it's so dirty and dangerous. I only ever take taxis."

Well la-di-freakin'-da! I would completely agree with you that the NYC subway is unsafe, if we were in 1985. And dirty? You think taxis are any cleaner? My grandfather drove a taxi for 40 years in the city and told me he always had to carry towels with him while he was on duty...you know, to clean up. If you believe taxis are any cleaner, I got one word for you... blacklight.

Even though the conversation continued beyond the taxi comment, I realized this fare had reached its destination. It was the way she talked about her life. She wanted to end up with a 6'2" financial guy with 34 custom suits and a Maserati. I'm 5'8" and my "suits" are no more than matching pants and jackets with a tie. The only form of transportation I have, beyond public and my legs, is a mountain bike that has gathered an extremely impressive layer of dust. I'm not against taking a taxi, but there are many times the subway is much faster. Like when the president comes to town. Please, stop coming to NYC.

Part of her reasoning for only taking a taxi was because she always wore heels. Heels. Really? 'Cause no other woman on the NYC subway system wears heels. Wait a second, yes they do! They may wear sneakers for half the journey, but damned if I've seen them change while on the subway preparing for the morning rush.

Conversation ended amicably, though. We wished each other a good weekend and to enjoy the upcoming holiday. I realized baby naming was not in our future.

Hey Hack, *Check Please!*

Gravy NY
32 East 21st St
New York, NY
212-600-2105

Table #109
4979   Serv: Adam
2011 9:27 PM   # Cust:0

an Descript   Cost

Glass Cote du Rhone $10.00
Gl Mcwilliams Shiraz $10.00
Gl Alto 3 Cabernet $13.00
Corn Flake Crusted Chic $21.00
Scallops & Grits $24.00

Net Total: $78.00
Tax $6.92

TOTAL: $84.92
Amount Due: $84.92
Visit us online
Gravyny.com

s#:
2011 9:27 PM

Reservoir Bar
70 University Place
New York, NY 10003
212-475-0770

43   04/20/11-A   6:57pm
PM BARTENDER Table (STANDEE)
END COUPLE

SALSA & GUAC
UESADILLA   3.95
                   7.50

Server 10 Noon-W

Red Green Salad   6.00
gherita Pizza   14.00
ta   6.00
Brothers Cane & Abel 7.00

Taxable: 33.00
Sub-total: 33.00
Tax: 2.93

Total Due: 35.93

someone who
couldn't make it to Motorino? Know
Motorino to them with
a pizza to-go.

d for Choosing Motorino! Know

Salsa & Guac

Red Green Salad   36.00
                      36.00
Items
Tax   3.20
TOTAL   39.20

ABOUT OUR WEEKEND WINE SCHOOLS AND
FREE PANINI MONDAYS!!!!
THANK YOU!
VERO UPTOWN

-CETAMURA

Rec: 11
54, Swiped T: 998 Term: 1

Total: 74.04
Tax: 6.04
        68.00

55.

31.57

Duplicate Copy****

OLDER WILL PAY CARD ISSUER ABOVE
T PURSUANT TO CARDHOLDER AGREEMENT

TIP:

Duplicate Copy****

ACCOUNT NUMBER
XXXXXXXXXX
XXXX

REN BAYROFF
TION APPROVED

Credit Card SALE

Ave
NY 10021

"You're too DUMB for me"

"I'll take 'spell your own name' for $400, Alex."

That's not exactly what she said, but it was damn close. She and I had gone out on many dates, stayed at each other's apartments, dinner, movies, all of it. We never discussed labels, kept everything very loose, until I sent one very benign text message: *"Hey, how are you? You free this Friday? Thinking some Italian food. Let me know if you're free."*

Didn't hear from her for a couple of days. A phone call and another text, still nothing. We finally talked and she confessed she backed off because I recommended we go out on Friday, which is planet-wide known as "date night." That was a bit too serious for her. Honestly, I give Friday no more weight than any other day. Actually, I give more thought to which pair of shoes I wear than to what day of the week I ask someone out. (Tonight I am sitting at my computer wearing comfy flip flops.)

It was then I started wondering if I had secretly been dating a guy all this time. But I thought no. She always put the seat down and knew way too much about current sales at Sephora. To make matters worse (for me) she says: "It probably wasn't going to work out anyway. I'm not Jewish, I don't want kids, and then there's the intellectual difference."

Money
The number one relationship argument

Excuse me? Back up the insult trolley for a sec. "Intellectual difference?" For those who have met me, true, I'm not the sharpest knife in the drawer. But I can finish at least ¼ of the NY Times Crossword, and get a minimum of 10 answers correct on Jeopardy within a three week period. Far from a genius, yet leagues away from sitting in the corner eating paste.

She didn't quantify her remark, she simply said goodbye and that was that. So, I immediately took the practice Mensa test online, to prove her wrong. My score was an icon laughing at me while pointing its finger.

Mr. Berrill, Dr. Ware, *Check Please!*

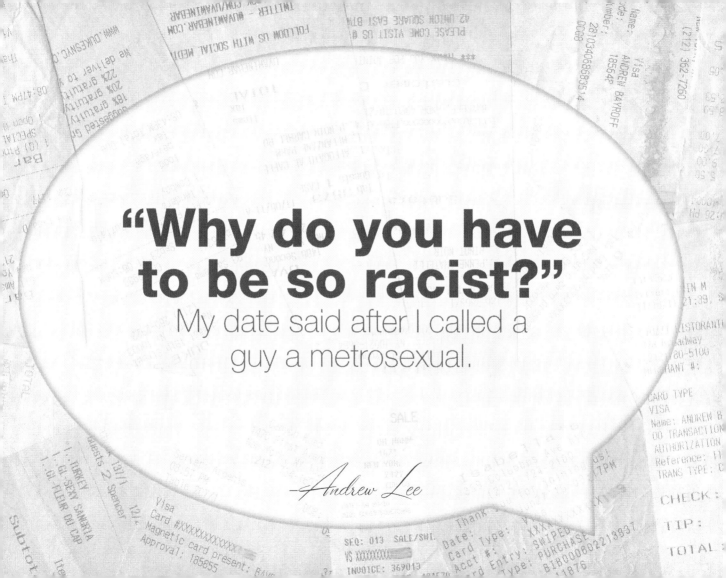

"Oh, you've never **HEARD** of me?"

"*You'll need to sign this Non Disclosure Agreement before the date begins.*"

This story takes us back a few years. Midday, Los Angeles, and of course, it was beautiful weather. It was LA. Anything below 78 degrees in LA is considered potential frostbite.

I can't remember her exact order, but it went something like: "I'd like a Venti quad-shot, half-caff, low-foam, 2 pumps of Vanilla, room for milk." I ordered a regular coffee and a muffin.

Her order reminded me of the Steve Martin move *LA Story*:
Tom: *I'll have a decaf coffee.*
Trudi: *I'll have a decaf espresso.*
Morris Frost: *I'll have a double decaf cappuccino.*
Ted: *Give me decaffeinated coffee ice cream.*
Harris: *I'll have a half double decaffeinated half-caff, with a twist of lemon.*
Trudi: *I'll have a twist of lemon.*
Tom: *I'll have a twist of lemon.*
Morris Frost: *I'll have a twist of lemon.*
Cynthia: *I'll have a twist of lemon.*

As we sat down and started to chat, she handed me one of her business cards. When my face showed no sense of recognition, surprise or awe, she awkwardly offered, "I can't believe you haven't heard of me. I'm a manager of a couple of big names in LA." When asked, she couldn't tell me whom she managed, because, "contracts have not been signed yet." I was thinking, "Is that because they haven't heard of you either?"

The conversation consisted of her asking me questions and how my answers pertained to her and her life. "During the day I'm a designer, at night I take improv classes at The Groundlings and perform stand up," I said, to which she responded, "Stand up, I love stand up. I almost represented a really big name years ago, I wish I could tell you who."

My attempts at pushing the conversation away from entertainment was met with a concrete blockade. She was either incapable of talking about anything but entertainment, or knew nothing else. It was LA. The hint of even an imaginary client is worth talking about.

As the coffee disappeared so did the conversation; we proceeded to the end of the script on our first date. She gave me a suspended air cheek kiss, turned and walked away. Exit stage...oh, who the hell cares.

Barista! *Check Please!*

A girl on a date once:

"I have herpes, but it's not active right now."

—Mick Diflo

Tbl 24/1
Jan18'10 03:12PM   Chk 5976

1 CHICKEN SANDW
1 MEDITERRANEA
1 ADD SHRIMP

food
Tax
03:55PM Total Due

Thank you for your patronage a
ARTE CAFE
For reservations please call
212-501-7014
For complaints or suggestions
please call Victor 646-241-939

27.

SEP 22.10   APPROVAL
                141647
ANDREW BAYROFF
****
VISA   *****
        SALE   0001
ROC #   TERMINAL #
430470   27701639
FOOD AND BEVERAGE
BASE AMOUNT $23.55
TIP AMOUNT   _____
TOTAL   _____

I AGREE TO PAY ABOVE TOTAL AMOUNT
ACCORDING TO CARD ISSUER AGREEMENT
(MERCHANT AGREEMENT IF CREDIT VOUCHER)
CUSTOMER COPY

CUSTOMER COPY

CUSTOMER COPY

Wine & Roses
286 Columbus Avenue
NY NY 10023
212-579-WINE

05/12/2010 07:09PM

0103 Barbaresco
0101 Cab.Sav
2 Encanadas

SUBTOTAL
Tax
Incl Tax

TOTAL DUE

Thank You

>>Customer Copy<<
Side Bar - 212.277.2900
Vintage Irving - 212.677.5300

Thank You!

**Le Pain
Quotidien**
1270 First Ave
New York NY 105
(212)-988-500
Oct08'11

Date:
Card Type: visa
Acct #:   XXXXXXXX
Card Entry: SWIPED
Trans Type: PURCHAS
Trans Key: CIC005
Auth Code: 165117
Check: 1971
Server: 5548 Pamela P

20.10

Thank you for choosi
Le Pain Quotid

Catering and Gro
Delivery Available-Pleas
1-855-TARTINE (827-84

**NO SIGNATURE
REQUIRED Merc**

TOTAL AMOUNT

BOAT BASIN
side and 79th St
New   10
212.4

TAL $
TIP $
OTAL $

======
STOMER C Total
****

& Roses
Columbus Avenue
NY NY 10023
212-579-WINE

05/12/2010 08:21PM
Visa
****
++/++
162222
1454
25-1
203 Tex
er: 013300603622

Bar Luna
511 Amsterdam Ave
New York NY 10024
212-362-1098

Cnk 2200
Sep22'10 07:27PM Gst 2

Dr.
Noir

14.00
11.00
0.00
15.00

40.00
3.55
____
43.55

dining with us!

GRACIE M
1550 1
NEW YORK
212-86
MID 38590

Merchant ID: 028100
Term ID: 001

Sa

XXXXXXXXXX
VISA

11/13/11
Inv #: 000204
Apprvd: Online

Amount:
Tip:

Total:

)-229-0222
13th Stree
rk, NY 1001

Server: Marlissa
08:33 PM
Table 22/1

Visa
Card #XXXXXXXXXXX
Magnetic card present
Approval #: 183233

= Total: _____
+ Tip: _____

X

"I'm looking for someone to TAKE CARE of me"

yet another...

"Sweetie. What do you say we skip the picnic and go straight to you bottle feeding me?"

This one went well past the first date, however, the ending is one of my favorites.

She was attractive, smart, witty, and sarcastic. She could have been my Liz Lemon. We hit it off as soon as we met and things went uphill from there, until a little more than month into dating she tells me, "Andrew, I think I need to tell you that I'm looking for someone to take care of me."

Oy, not again.

She continues: "I'm a 37-year old female and have been taking care of myself my entire adult life. I'm looking for someone to take care of me now."

There's a reason you've been taking care of yourself sweetness. You're an adult. That's what adults do! We take care of ourselves. And for the record, men don't automatically get a raise at work when we start dating someone. I don't have a 6-month sex review with my boss: "Well, Andrew, it says here you've been getting some lately. Here's a 5% raise, keep hitting that." I so wish it worked that way, but sadly, all requests in the "Suggestions Box" at work have gone unanswered.

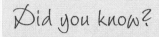*Did you know?*

In American society, when a man offers his date his palm face up, he is most likely deeply attracted to the woman.

Talking to a bartender makes a woman seem more friendly and makes it easier for a guy to jump in on her conversation.

Italian food is one of the most popular restaurants for a first date.

50%
New York state adults that are unmarried

She then went on to tell me that men should pay on dates, because, "Not only do women make 80% of what men do, but women have the added cost of hair, nails, makeup, clothing, and waxing." Yes, because if it weren't for men, women would have unkempt hair, long nails, and leg hair long enough to braid. Somehow, I have to think women primp, pluck, and prepare to show off in front of other women as well.

So to prove to her I was up for the challenge, and to show her how much she meant to me, I planned a picnic in Central Park. Even though it rained the day of, no worries, I brought the picnic into my apartment. Blanket, wine, and a spread of cheeses, meats, veggies and dip. I had her close her eyes when she walked into my apartment, brought her closer to the center of the room, and as soon as she opened her eyes, her first words were: "You know I ate already, right?"

Jesus Christ. How about a thank you!

About a week or so later we "ended it all" over Facebook instant messenger. Classy, ey?

Excuse me, Mr. Zuckerberg, *Check Please!*

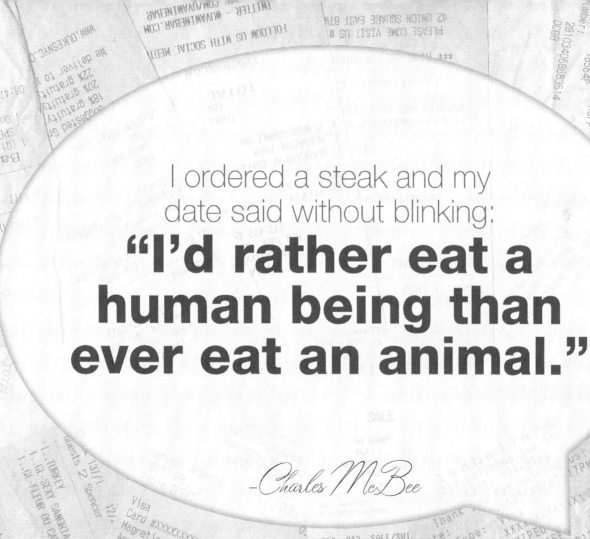

Cust#WALK-IN   Jul 09 10
HOU Rg#134 Dr#134 Time 07:24

Qty   Price   Ext

1   10.99Y   10.99
.68   5A
.11   6.99N   .11
.98   10.99N
LB   1.21
19.29
20.00

Openers 8am-8:30pm Every Day
Cater Your Next Event!
Made Gift Baskets.

Belmont Lounge
www.BelmontLoungeNYC.com
117 East 15 Street
New York, NY, 10003

Server: Zhanna
Table 106/1
Guests: 2

Order Type: Send

1940's Champagne Julep
Gls Cabernet Lyeth

Subtotal

Total   Balance Due

$51.80

(212) 593-2223

DOB: 12/31/2010
12/31/2010
1/10107   1048619

:er: BAR #1
38 PM
107/1

Amount: 35.93

gnetic card present: BAYROFF ANDREW
rd #XXXXXXXXXX
proval: 193385

+ Tip: _____

= Total: _____

GUESTS COPY

Felice is now open for Lunch
Mon - Fri and Sat - Sun brunch
20% automatic gratuity for
parties of six or more
Thank You!!!

AMERICAN TRASH

Date: 7/4/2010   Time: 2:37:05 AM

Status: Approved

Card Type: Visa
Card Number: XXXXXXXXXXXX1039
Expiration Date: XX/XX/XXXX
Swipe/Manual: Swipe
Server ID: 11
Server Name: Ian 2
Check Number: 94625
6834

Side Bar
Vintage Irving
120 East 15th Street
New York, NY 10003

Server: Marissa
Table 22/1
Guests: 1

Cabernet GLS
Quesadilla
  Chicken
Shock Top DRF

Complete Subtotal

Subtotal
Tax

---

ndmare [time warner center]
10 Columbus Circle
New York, NY 10019

ALLISON
12/03/2010   10064
10:40 PM

29.00   10.00
4.00   10.00

53.00
4.70

57.70   57.70

nce Due

for information about
private events or catering
please call
212.625.8270
thank you

teak
s
mes
Subtotal

older bayroff/and
umber XXXXXXXXXX
Code: 151587

ount...
Tip....

2-70

"Hi, it's Andrew.
WHERE
are you?"

*"Andrew, you never told me **which** tree to meet you near."*

This was the voicemail I left for a woman I was supposedly meeting downtown. She never showed. Rather, she never even attempted.

A day before, she and I agreed on meeting at a predetermined subway stop in lower Manhattan, then finding a bar from there. I arrived at 6:30 P.M., a little early actually. Five minutes passed, then 15, then 25, then 30. I sent two text messages and left two voice messages.

I finally hopped back on the subway and headed home, not quite understanding what had happened. I finally heard from her, over an hour later. She told me she was waiting to hear from me about a place to meet. When she never heard from me, she simply went home after work. This, after a specific conversation about that we'd meet first, and walk from there.

I asked her: "So, instead of maybe calling me, you went home?" She had no real answer. She said the "blame" was on both of us. I did not agree, since she couldn't even reach out and call me, God forbid! "The phone...it's so heavy...can't...pick it...up...and dial...your number." (Your best impression of William Shatner would be most appreciated.)

Did you know?

A recent AOL survey says that 40% of women view an appropriate time frame to wait for sex is one to three months, while 35% of men think the third date is fine.

Twenty to 40 million Americans have used online dating services.

On Match.com, 132 million winks are sent out each year and members go out on a six million dates per year.

17%

The chance that some will like a date set up by a friend

We rescheduled the date for following week, but this time we chose a specific place. A cool little coffee house we would both enjoy. The day finally came and she didn't show up, again. I first checked the time. All good. The place? Correct address. After I texted her, she told me she didn't think the date was on since I failed (failed!) to reconfirm the day of. I wasn't aware that you needed to reconfirm in 24 hour increments. Silly me.

Not allowing her to spoil two dates in a row, I sat and ate two pastries and drank two coffees. That'll show her!

And for those of you who think she was simply trying to blow me off, she contacted me a month later and did the same exact thing again. So shame on those of you for thinking it was me. But kudos for those of you who called me an ass for going the third time.

Excuse me, Magellan, *Check Please!*

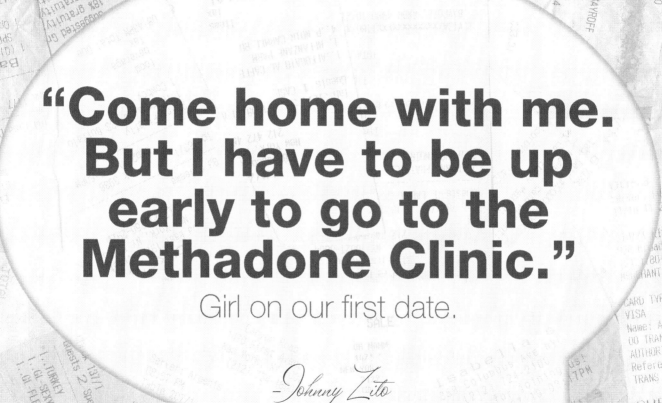

"Why would you DO THAT to a little person?"

"Normally, I don't do this on the first date, but you seem special."

**F**irst off, I didn't do a thing to anyone, little or not. That said...

I met this woman, yes, online. Emails turned into a phone call, which led to a first date, which is when the wheels and doors came off the car. As well as the muffler, rear view mirrors, and oil pan.

We were both very much attracted to each other as soon as we met at our Upper West Side wine bar. Light talking led to deeper discussion, us holding hands, then to a beautiful kiss at the bar. Things were going well.

We were now into the second hour of our first date, feeling high on wine, and attraction. What I perceived to be a spark between us was simply the soon-to-be charred odor of the carcass of our date.

As we transitioned from the bar to outside, we tried to decide what to do, since the night was still early. I—and this where the oil hit the water—suggested in my three part stand up routine:

"Well, we can walk in Central Park, grab some coffee, or maybe go midget tossing." Suffice to say, the look on her face was less than pleased. I know this because I was there, witnessing the horror

40mil

Number of Americans who use online dating services

painted across her face. She stopped walking and turned towards me, "Why on earth would you even suggest something like that? Why would you do that to a little person?"

Indeed, why would I say something like that? Maybe because I had just seen a TV report about midget tossing the night before[4]. However, let me be perfectly clear: I am not endorsing, advocating, promoting, or in any way, shape, or form declaring little person tossing an acceptable first date activity.

I was able to salvage a tiny bit of the same magic we had no less than 30 seconds prior. Alas, it was not meant to be. She's actually a mom now. So she now has her very own "little" person.

There's no place like home, *Check Please!*

" I have a security clearance HIGHER than a general "

"I think I'd know if it weren't safe to parachute into the Middle East, Andrew!"

Unfortunately, our conversation in the East Village swayed towards politics and government right away. And anyone that has made that mistake knows that path is filled with wine bar IEDs.

Plus, she seemed like a very militant Jew, and with just one word against Israel, or dreidels, she would spontaneously combust...into a thousand smaller versions of herself which would suffocate you with all of their tiny, tiny hands.

Here's how the conversation went:

I started off by saying, "I don't mind shrinking our military, just as long as we keep our covert operations active. Need to keep watch on certain people."

"What do you mean covert operations?" she said, furrowing her brow, looking directly at me.

"You know, the military personnel no one really knows about. Planted in various countries." I tapped my nose, wink wink.

Smirking, she declares, "I have a Level 20 security clearance, Andrew, higher than a general. I think I would know if the US government is doing that sort of thing."

My own brow became permanently furrowed for the rest of the night. Mind you, I wasn't fighting her, just stating the obvious. We may not have Jason Bourne planted in an Iraqi village, but at least a Monk or a Columbo. Let's face it, I'd be happy with Mr. Bean.

She negated me for the next 45 minutes on, well, most every topic we landed on. Politics, religion, children, and whether or not Mac is better than PC. Making disparaging comments about the Mac to me is akin to talking about Fight Club. And as we all know, you don't talk about Fight Club!

As the night drew to a thankful close, we both realized we would never own a his-and-hers retina scanning booth.

The eagle has left the wine bar, *Check Please!*

On a date, I said, "I'm hungry. You want to get something to eat?"

"Sure. There's a Kentucky Fried Chicken near by."

I paid for my half.

—Julie Kottakis

"It will be more CONVENIENT for me"

"As you can clearly see, I have a 25′ dating radius. I will not be taking any questions."

I like to think I'm the type of guy who will find a first date spot that is either near the girl's apartment or where she works.

On the phone getting to know one another, she said she was a school teacher and avid gym girl. When I asked her what day would work best for her, she responded Saturday. Good. Great. I can work with Saturday. And on a side note, that's really all a guy is looks for. An "in." Give a guy at least a day you're available and we're happier than fifty pigs in shit.

However, ladies, there are times you can give too much information, request too much. Like the kid who just got the new Xbox and still yells at his mother—in the store—because she didn't get the exact games he told her to buy.

My soon-to-be first date continued by saying: "If we can also do it around 8 P.M., and I like wine bars, and since I'll be at the gym beforehand, can we make it my neighborhood? It'll just be more convenient for me."

Is there anything else you will require mum? Perhaps a soft pillow for your feet? Or maybe a butler to wipe your...anyway. Far be it from me to request she goes a single train stop to meet me. I said,

"OK, no problem. Can you recommend any place in your neighborhood?" To which she responded, "No, not really. Anything you find is fine."

So we're not only meeting on her day, her time, *and* in her neighborhood, she couldn't even recommend one single place? Women, you may pay a lot for makeup, a blow out, mani/pedi, and that sexy strapless dress, but don't think for a moment men don't jump through some courting hoops themselves.

I chose a wine bar, on a Saturday, in her neighborhood, at 8 P.M. She was late. By 20 minutes. She said the bar wasn't as close to her apt as she would have liked. Off to a great start!

We chatted for a while, glass of wine each. We both talked about where we were from, what we do, and projects we were working on. She reminded me a few times that she was indeed a real blonde, and did not use any fake color, but that her mother did from time to time. All interesting information, if we were at a salon, and if I didn't stop listening 25 minutes ago.

Just rinse, oh, and, *Check Please!*

Guy: "I wished we talked more, but then I look at you and I want to have sex".

"Which I might have gone for had the sex been better!"

-Michelle McGill

The Romantic

The Deep Thinker

The Communicator

The Investigator

The Hall of Dates

The Traditional

The Clean

The Considerate

The Petrified

The Delusional

The Patient

The Touchy-Feely

The Foodie

The Pungent

The Hall of Dates

The Absent

The Navigator

The Idiot

The Precise

The Informed

Don't wait three days

Unlike the dating rule, I want to hear from you today! Visit us at www.CheckPleaseBook.com and click on the blog link to post your own dating story and share it with the world. I hope you enjoyed reading the book as much as I did writing it.

References

[1] "Did You Know" side bar stats

http://facts.randomhistory.com/dating-and-relationship-facts.html

[2] "Did You Know" side bar bottom "crown" stats

http://www.statisticbrain.com/dating-relationship-stats/

[3] First Date prices

http://gothamist.com/2011/06/12/new_yorkers_dont_spend_enough_on_fi.php

[4] http://en.wikipedia.org/wiki/Dwarf_tossing

Quick Quotes
Supplied from friends and comics of the author. Full release obtained.

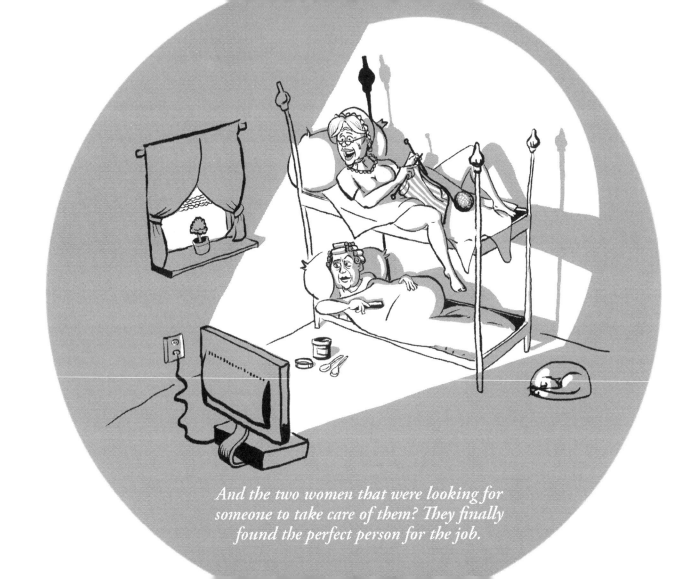

And the two women that were looking for someone to take care of them? They finally found the perfect person for the job.

Made in the USA
Charleston, SC
22 October 2014